50 Homemade Pizza Recipes to Try at Home

By: Kelly Johnson

Table of Contents

- Margherita Pizza
- Pepperoni Pizza
- Veggie Supreme Pizza
- BBQ Chicken Pizza
- Hawaiian Pizza
- Four Cheese Pizza
- Meat Lover's Pizza
- White Garlic Pizza
- Buffalo Chicken Pizza
- Margherita with Pesto Pizza
- Sausage and Peppers Pizza
- Mediterranean Pizza with Olives and Feta
- BBQ Pulled Pork Pizza
- Chicken Alfredo Pizza
- Caprese Pizza
- Spinach and Ricotta Pizza
- Bacon and Egg Breakfast Pizza
- Pesto and Mozzarella Pizza
- Chicken Caesar Salad Pizza
- Pepperoni and Mushroom Pizza
- Shrimp Scampi Pizza
- Philly Cheesesteak Pizza
- Mushroom and Truffle Oil Pizza
- Taco Pizza
- Chicken Parmesan Pizza
- Philly Chicken Pizza
- Bacon, Lettuce, and Tomato Pizza
- Smoked Salmon Pizza
- Taco Supreme Pizza
- Artichoke and Spinach Pizza
- Clam Pizza
- Focaccia-Style Pizza
- Mediterranean Veggie Pizza
- Meatball Pizza
- Prosciutto and Arugula Pizza

- Sweet and Spicy Pineapple Pizza
- Zucchini and Feta Pizza
- BBQ Bacon Cheeseburger Pizza
- Roasted Veggie Pizza
- Steak and Gorgonzola Pizza
- Eggplant Parmesan Pizza
- Ricotta and Sausage Pizza
- Gorgonzola, Pear, and Walnut Pizza
- Balsamic Glazed Onion Pizza
- Fig and Prosciutto Pizza
- Goat Cheese and Caramelized Onion Pizza
- Roasted Garlic and Herb Pizza
- Pesto Chicken and Sun-Dried Tomato Pizza
- Roasted Beetroot and Goat Cheese Pizza
- Truffle Mushroom Pizza

Margherita Pizza

Ingredients:

- 1 pizza dough (store-bought or homemade)
- 1/2 cup pizza sauce
- 1 1/2 cups fresh mozzarella cheese, sliced
- Fresh basil leaves
- 1 tbsp olive oil
- Salt and pepper to taste

Instructions:

1. **Preheat the oven**: Preheat to 475°F (245°C). If using a pizza stone, preheat it in the oven.
2. **Assemble the pizza**: Roll out the pizza dough onto a lightly floured surface. Spread a thin layer of pizza sauce over the dough. Top with sliced mozzarella.
3. **Bake**: Bake for 10-12 minutes, until the crust is golden and the cheese is bubbly.
4. **Finish the pizza**: After baking, top with fresh basil leaves. Drizzle with olive oil and season with salt and pepper.
5. **Serve**: Slice and enjoy!

Pepperoni Pizza

Ingredients:

- 1 pizza dough
- 1/2 cup pizza sauce
- 1 1/2 cups shredded mozzarella cheese
- 1/2 cup pepperoni slices
- 1 tsp dried oregano

Instructions:

1. **Preheat the oven**: Preheat to 475°F (245°C).
2. **Assemble the pizza**: Roll out the pizza dough and spread pizza sauce over it. Sprinkle mozzarella cheese evenly on top. Arrange pepperoni slices over the cheese.
3. **Bake**: Bake for 10-12 minutes, until the crust is golden and cheese is melted.
4. **Finish the pizza**: Sprinkle with dried oregano.
5. **Serve**: Slice and enjoy!

Veggie Supreme Pizza

Ingredients:

- 1 pizza dough
- 1/2 cup pizza sauce
- 1 1/2 cups shredded mozzarella cheese
- 1/2 cup sliced bell peppers
- 1/4 cup red onion, thinly sliced
- 1/2 cup mushrooms, sliced
- 1/4 cup black olives, sliced
- 1/2 cup spinach leaves
- 1 tsp dried oregano

Instructions:

1. **Preheat the oven**: Preheat to 475°F (245°C).
2. **Assemble the pizza**: Roll out the pizza dough and spread pizza sauce over it. Add shredded mozzarella cheese evenly. Top with bell peppers, red onion, mushrooms, olives, and spinach.
3. **Bake**: Bake for 10-12 minutes until the crust is golden and the cheese is melted.
4. **Finish the pizza**: Sprinkle with dried oregano.
5. **Serve**: Slice and enjoy!

BBQ Chicken Pizza

Ingredients:

- 1 pizza dough
- 1/2 cup BBQ sauce
- 1 1/2 cups cooked chicken breast, shredded
- 1 1/2 cups shredded mozzarella cheese
- 1/4 cup red onion, thinly sliced
- 1/4 cup cilantro, chopped

Instructions:

1. **Preheat the oven**: Preheat to 475°F (245°C).
2. **Assemble the pizza**: Roll out the pizza dough and spread BBQ sauce over it. Add shredded mozzarella cheese evenly, followed by shredded chicken and red onion slices.
3. **Bake**: Bake for 10-12 minutes until the crust is golden and the cheese is melted.
4. **Finish the pizza**: Sprinkle with chopped cilantro.
5. **Serve**: Slice and enjoy!

Hawaiian Pizza

Ingredients:

- 1 pizza dough
- 1/2 cup pizza sauce
- 1 1/2 cups shredded mozzarella cheese
- 1/2 cup pineapple chunks
- 1/2 cup cooked ham, diced
- 1 tsp dried oregano

Instructions:

1. **Preheat the oven**: Preheat to 475°F (245°C).
2. **Assemble the pizza**: Roll out the pizza dough and spread pizza sauce over it. Add shredded mozzarella cheese evenly, then top with pineapple chunks and diced ham.
3. **Bake**: Bake for 10-12 minutes until the crust is golden and the cheese is bubbly.
4. **Finish the pizza**: Sprinkle with dried oregano.
5. **Serve**: Slice and enjoy!

Four Cheese Pizza

Ingredients:

- 1 pizza dough
- 1/2 cup pizza sauce
- 1/2 cup shredded mozzarella cheese
- 1/2 cup ricotta cheese
- 1/4 cup grated Parmesan cheese
- 1/4 cup crumbled blue cheese
- Fresh basil leaves for garnish (optional)

Instructions:

1. **Preheat the oven**: Preheat to 475°F (245°C).
2. **Assemble the pizza**: Roll out the pizza dough and spread a thin layer of pizza sauce over it. Top with mozzarella, ricotta, Parmesan, and blue cheese.
3. **Bake**: Bake for 10-12 minutes until the crust is golden and the cheese is melted and bubbly.
4. **Finish the pizza**: Garnish with fresh basil leaves if desired.
5. **Serve**: Slice and enjoy!

Meat Lover's Pizza

Ingredients:

- 1 pizza dough
- 1/2 cup pizza sauce
- 1 1/2 cups shredded mozzarella cheese
- 1/2 cup cooked sausage, crumbled
- 1/2 cup pepperoni slices
- 1/2 cup cooked bacon, crumbled
- 1/4 cup cooked ground beef
- 1 tsp dried oregano

Instructions:

1. **Preheat the oven**: Preheat to 475°F (245°C).
2. **Assemble the pizza**: Roll out the pizza dough and spread pizza sauce over it. Add shredded mozzarella cheese evenly. Layer with sausage, pepperoni, bacon, and ground beef.
3. **Bake**: Bake for 10-12 minutes until the crust is golden and the cheese is melted.
4. **Finish the pizza**: Sprinkle with dried oregano.
5. **Serve**: Slice and enjoy!

White Garlic Pizza

Ingredients:

- 1 pizza dough
- 1/2 cup ricotta cheese
- 1/2 cup shredded mozzarella cheese
- 2 tbsp olive oil
- 3 cloves garlic, minced
- 1/4 cup Parmesan cheese
- Fresh parsley for garnish (optional)
- Salt and pepper to taste

Instructions:

1. **Preheat the oven**: Preheat to 475°F (245°C).
2. **Assemble the pizza**: Roll out the pizza dough and spread a thin layer of ricotta cheese over it. Top with mozzarella cheese, minced garlic, and Parmesan.
3. **Bake**: Drizzle with olive oil and bake for 10-12 minutes until the crust is golden and the cheese is melted.
4. **Finish the pizza**: Garnish with fresh parsley and season with salt and pepper.
5. **Serve**: Slice and enjoy!

Buffalo Chicken Pizza

Ingredients:

- 1 pizza dough
- 1/2 cup buffalo sauce
- 1 1/2 cups cooked chicken breast, shredded
- 1 1/2 cups shredded mozzarella cheese
- 1/4 cup blue cheese crumbles
- 1/4 cup celery, finely chopped (optional)
- 1 tbsp olive oil
- Salt and pepper to taste

Instructions:

1. **Preheat the oven**: Preheat to 475°F (245°C).
2. **Assemble the pizza**: Roll out the pizza dough and spread buffalo sauce over it. Layer with shredded mozzarella and shredded chicken. Sprinkle with blue cheese crumbles.
3. **Bake**: Bake for 10-12 minutes until the crust is golden and cheese is melted.
4. **Finish the pizza**: Drizzle with a bit more buffalo sauce and sprinkle chopped celery for crunch.
5. **Serve**: Slice and enjoy!

Margherita with Pesto Pizza

Ingredients:

- 1 pizza dough
- 1/2 cup pizza sauce
- 1/4 cup pesto sauce
- 1 1/2 cups fresh mozzarella cheese, sliced
- Fresh basil leaves
- 1 tbsp olive oil
- Salt and pepper to taste

Instructions:

1. **Preheat the oven**: Preheat to 475°F (245°C).
2. **Assemble the pizza**: Roll out the pizza dough and spread a layer of pizza sauce. Add a layer of pesto sauce on top. Place the mozzarella slices evenly.
3. **Bake**: Bake for 10-12 minutes until the crust is golden and the cheese is bubbly.
4. **Finish the pizza**: Top with fresh basil leaves. Drizzle with olive oil and season with salt and pepper.
5. **Serve**: Slice and enjoy!

Sausage and Peppers Pizza

Ingredients:

- 1 pizza dough
- 1/2 cup pizza sauce
- 1 1/2 cups shredded mozzarella cheese
- 1/2 lb Italian sausage, crumbled and cooked
- 1/2 cup bell peppers, thinly sliced
- 1/4 cup onions, thinly sliced
- 1 tbsp olive oil
- 1 tsp dried oregano

Instructions:

1. **Preheat the oven**: Preheat to 475°F (245°C).
2. **Assemble the pizza**: Roll out the pizza dough and spread pizza sauce over it. Add mozzarella cheese evenly, then top with crumbled sausage, bell peppers, and onions.
3. **Bake**: Bake for 10-12 minutes until the crust is golden and the cheese is melted.
4. **Finish the pizza**: Drizzle with olive oil and sprinkle dried oregano.
5. **Serve**: Slice and enjoy!

Mediterranean Pizza with Olives and Feta

Ingredients:

- 1 pizza dough
- 1/2 cup pizza sauce
- 1 1/2 cups shredded mozzarella cheese
- 1/2 cup black olives, sliced
- 1/4 cup red onion, thinly sliced
- 1/2 cup feta cheese, crumbled
- 1/4 cup spinach leaves
- 1 tsp dried oregano

Instructions:

1. **Preheat the oven**: Preheat to 475°F (245°C).
2. **Assemble the pizza**: Roll out the pizza dough and spread pizza sauce. Add mozzarella cheese, then top with olives, red onion, feta, and spinach.
3. **Bake**: Bake for 10-12 minutes until the crust is golden and the cheese is melted.
4. **Finish the pizza**: Sprinkle with dried oregano.
5. **Serve**: Slice and enjoy!

BBQ Pulled Pork Pizza

Ingredients:

- 1 pizza dough
- 1/2 cup BBQ sauce
- 1 1/2 cups pulled pork (cooked)
- 1 1/2 cups shredded mozzarella cheese
- 1/4 cup red onion, thinly sliced
- 1 tbsp cilantro, chopped
- 1 tbsp olive oil

Instructions:

1. **Preheat the oven**: Preheat to 475°F (245°C).
2. **Assemble the pizza**: Roll out the pizza dough and spread BBQ sauce over it. Layer with pulled pork and mozzarella cheese. Top with red onion slices.
3. **Bake**: Bake for 10-12 minutes until the crust is golden and cheese is melted.
4. **Finish the pizza**: Drizzle with olive oil and sprinkle chopped cilantro.
5. **Serve**: Slice and enjoy!

Chicken Alfredo Pizza

Ingredients:

- 1 pizza dough
- 1/2 cup Alfredo sauce
- 1 1/2 cups cooked chicken breast, shredded
- 1 1/2 cups shredded mozzarella cheese
- 1/4 cup Parmesan cheese, grated
- 1/4 cup spinach leaves (optional)

Instructions:

1. **Preheat the oven**: Preheat to 475°F (245°C).
2. **Assemble the pizza**: Roll out the pizza dough and spread Alfredo sauce. Add shredded mozzarella and top with chicken and Parmesan.
3. **Bake**: Bake for 10-12 minutes until the crust is golden and the cheese is melted.
4. **Finish the pizza**: Add spinach leaves for extra flavor (optional).
5. **Serve**: Slice and enjoy!

Caprese Pizza

Ingredients:

- 1 pizza dough
- 1/2 cup pizza sauce
- 1 1/2 cups fresh mozzarella cheese, sliced
- 1/2 cup cherry tomatoes, halved
- Fresh basil leaves
- 1 tbsp balsamic glaze
- 1 tbsp olive oil

Instructions:

1. **Preheat the oven**: Preheat to 475°F (245°C).
2. **Assemble the pizza**: Roll out the pizza dough and spread pizza sauce over it. Place mozzarella slices and cherry tomatoes evenly on top.
3. **Bake**: Bake for 10-12 minutes until the crust is golden and cheese is melted.
4. **Finish the pizza**: Drizzle with balsamic glaze and olive oil. Top with fresh basil.
5. **Serve**: Slice and enjoy!

Spinach and Ricotta Pizza

Ingredients:

- 1 pizza dough
- 1/2 cup pizza sauce
- 1 1/2 cups fresh mozzarella cheese, shredded
- 1/2 cup ricotta cheese
- 1 cup spinach leaves, cooked and drained
- 1/4 cup Parmesan cheese, grated
- Salt and pepper to taste

Instructions:

1. **Preheat the oven**: Preheat to 475°F (245°C).
2. **Assemble the pizza**: Roll out the pizza dough and spread pizza sauce over it. Add mozzarella cheese and dollops of ricotta. Top with spinach and Parmesan.
3. **Bake**: Bake for 10-12 minutes until the crust is golden and the cheese is bubbly.
4. **Finish the pizza**: Season with salt and pepper.
5. **Serve**: Slice and enjoy!

Bacon and Egg Breakfast Pizza

Ingredients:

- 1 pizza dough
- 1/2 cup pizza sauce (optional)
- 1 1/2 cups shredded mozzarella cheese
- 4 slices bacon, cooked and crumbled
- 2 large eggs
- 1/4 cup green onions, chopped
- Salt and pepper to taste

Instructions:

1. **Preheat the oven**: Preheat to 475°F (245°C).
2. **Assemble the pizza**: Roll out the pizza dough and optionally spread pizza sauce. Top with mozzarella cheese, crumbled bacon, and green onions.
3. **Crack the eggs**: Make two small wells in the pizza and carefully crack the eggs into them.
4. **Bake**: Bake for 10-12 minutes until the crust is golden, cheese is melted, and the eggs are cooked to your desired doneness.
5. **Serve**: Sprinkle with salt and pepper, slice, and enjoy!

Pesto and Mozzarella Pizza

Ingredients:

- 1 pizza dough
- 1/2 cup pesto sauce
- 1 1/2 cups fresh mozzarella cheese, sliced
- 1/4 cup pine nuts (optional)
- Fresh basil leaves for garnish
- 1 tbsp olive oil

Instructions:

1. **Preheat the oven**: Preheat to 475°F (245°C).
2. **Assemble the pizza**: Roll out the pizza dough and spread a layer of pesto sauce. Add slices of mozzarella cheese.
3. **Bake**: Bake for 10-12 minutes until the crust is golden and the cheese is melted.
4. **Finish the pizza**: Sprinkle with pine nuts and drizzle with olive oil. Top with fresh basil leaves.
5. **Serve**: Slice and enjoy!

Chicken Caesar Salad Pizza

Ingredients:

- 1 pizza dough
- 1/2 cup Caesar dressing
- 1 1/2 cups cooked chicken breast, shredded
- 1 1/2 cups shredded mozzarella cheese
- 1/2 cup Parmesan cheese, grated
- 1/4 cup croutons
- Romaine lettuce, chopped
- Salt and pepper to taste

Instructions:

1. **Preheat the oven**: Preheat to 475°F (245°C).
2. **Assemble the pizza**: Roll out the pizza dough and spread Caesar dressing over the base. Add mozzarella cheese, then top with shredded chicken and Parmesan cheese.
3. **Bake**: Bake for 10-12 minutes until the crust is golden and the cheese is melted.
4. **Finish the pizza**: Once baked, top with chopped romaine lettuce, croutons, and extra Caesar dressing.
5. **Serve**: Slice and enjoy!

Pepperoni and Mushroom Pizza

Ingredients:

- 1 pizza dough
- 1/2 cup pizza sauce
- 1 1/2 cups shredded mozzarella cheese
- 1/2 cup pepperoni slices
- 1/2 cup mushrooms, sliced
- 1 tsp dried oregano

Instructions:

1. **Preheat the oven**: Preheat to 475°F (245°C).
2. **Assemble the pizza**: Roll out the pizza dough and spread pizza sauce. Layer with mozzarella cheese, pepperoni, and sliced mushrooms.
3. **Bake**: Bake for 10-12 minutes until the crust is golden and cheese is melted.
4. **Finish the pizza**: Sprinkle with dried oregano.
5. **Serve**: Slice and enjoy!

Shrimp Scampi Pizza

Ingredients:

- 1 pizza dough
- 1/2 cup Alfredo sauce
- 1 1/2 cups shredded mozzarella cheese
- 1/2 lb shrimp, peeled and deveined
- 2 cloves garlic, minced
- 1/4 cup parsley, chopped
- 1 tbsp olive oil
- Salt and pepper to taste

Instructions:

1. **Preheat the oven**: Preheat to 475°F (245°C).
2. **Sauté the shrimp**: Heat olive oil in a skillet over medium heat. Add minced garlic and shrimp, cooking until shrimp is pink and cooked through. Season with salt and pepper.
3. **Assemble the pizza**: Roll out the pizza dough and spread Alfredo sauce. Top with mozzarella cheese, sautéed shrimp, and garlic.
4. **Bake**: Bake for 10-12 minutes until the crust is golden and cheese is melted.
5. **Finish the pizza**: Sprinkle with fresh parsley.
6. **Serve**: Slice and enjoy!

Philly Cheesesteak Pizza

Ingredients:

- 1 pizza dough
- 1/2 cup pizza sauce (optional)
- 1 1/2 cups shredded mozzarella cheese
- 1/2 lb thinly sliced beef steak
- 1/2 cup green bell pepper, sliced
- 1/4 cup onions, thinly sliced
- 1 tbsp olive oil
- 1/4 cup provolone cheese, sliced

Instructions:

1. **Preheat the oven**: Preheat to 475°F (245°C).
2. **Sauté the beef**: Heat olive oil in a skillet and cook the beef until browned. Add bell pepper and onion slices, cooking until tender.
3. **Assemble the pizza**: Roll out the pizza dough and spread pizza sauce. Top with mozzarella cheese, cooked beef, peppers, and onions. Add slices of provolone on top.
4. **Bake**: Bake for 10-12 minutes until the crust is golden and cheese is melted.
5. **Serve**: Slice and enjoy!

Mushroom and Truffle Oil Pizza

Ingredients:

- 1 pizza dough
- 1/2 cup pizza sauce
- 1 1/2 cups fresh mozzarella cheese, sliced
- 1 cup mushrooms, sliced
- 1 tbsp truffle oil
- 1/4 cup Parmesan cheese, grated
- Fresh thyme leaves (optional)

Instructions:

1. **Preheat the oven**: Preheat to 475°F (245°C).
2. **Assemble the pizza**: Roll out the pizza dough and spread pizza sauce. Add mozzarella cheese and top with sliced mushrooms.
3. **Bake**: Bake for 10-12 minutes until the crust is golden and cheese is melted.
4. **Finish the pizza**: Drizzle with truffle oil, sprinkle with Parmesan cheese, and fresh thyme leaves.
5. **Serve**: Slice and enjoy!

Taco Pizza

Ingredients:

- 1 pizza dough
- 1/2 cup taco sauce
- 1 1/2 cups shredded cheddar cheese
- 1/2 lb ground beef, cooked and seasoned with taco seasoning
- 1/4 cup onions, finely chopped
- 1/4 cup black olives, sliced
- 1/2 cup shredded lettuce
- 1/4 cup tomatoes, chopped
- Sour cream and salsa (optional)

Instructions:

1. **Preheat the oven**: Preheat to 475°F (245°C).
2. **Assemble the pizza**: Roll out the pizza dough and spread taco sauce. Layer with cheddar cheese, then top with cooked ground beef, onions, and black olives.
3. **Bake**: Bake for 10-12 minutes until the crust is golden and cheese is melted.
4. **Finish the pizza**: After baking, top with shredded lettuce, chopped tomatoes, sour cream, and salsa if desired.
5. **Serve**: Slice and enjoy!

Chicken Parmesan Pizza

Ingredients:

- 1 pizza dough
- 1/2 cup marinara sauce
- 1 1/2 cups shredded mozzarella cheese
- 1/2 cup Parmesan cheese, grated
- 2 cooked chicken breasts, breaded and sliced
- 1/4 cup fresh basil leaves, chopped
- 1 tbsp olive oil

Instructions:

1. **Preheat the oven**: Preheat to 475°F (245°C).
2. **Assemble the pizza**: Roll out the pizza dough and spread marinara sauce. Add mozzarella cheese and top with Parmesan cheese. Layer the sliced chicken on top.
3. **Bake**: Bake for 10-12 minutes until the crust is golden and the cheese is bubbly.
4. **Finish the pizza**: Drizzle with olive oil and sprinkle with fresh basil.
5. **Serve**: Slice and enjoy!

Philly Chicken Pizza

Ingredients:

- 1 pizza dough
- 1/2 cup ranch dressing or pizza sauce
- 1 1/2 cups shredded mozzarella cheese
- 1/2 lb cooked chicken breast, thinly sliced
- 1/2 cup green bell pepper, sliced
- 1/4 cup red onion, sliced
- 1 tbsp olive oil
- Salt and pepper to taste

Instructions:

1. **Preheat the oven**: Preheat to 475°F (245°C).
2. **Sauté the veggies**: Heat olive oil in a pan and sauté bell peppers and onions until softened. Season with salt and pepper.
3. **Assemble the pizza**: Roll out the pizza dough and spread ranch dressing. Add mozzarella cheese, cooked chicken, sautéed veggies, and additional seasoning.
4. **Bake**: Bake for 10-12 minutes until the crust is golden and the cheese is melted.
5. **Serve**: Slice and enjoy!

Bacon, Lettuce, and Tomato Pizza

Ingredients:

- 1 pizza dough
- 1/2 cup pizza sauce
- 1 1/2 cups shredded mozzarella cheese
- 6 slices cooked bacon, crumbled
- 1/2 cup cherry tomatoes, halved
- 1/2 cup shredded lettuce
- 1 tbsp mayonnaise (optional)

Instructions:

1. **Preheat the oven**: Preheat to 475°F (245°C).
2. **Assemble the pizza**: Roll out the pizza dough and spread pizza sauce. Add mozzarella cheese and sprinkle with crumbled bacon and halved tomatoes.
3. **Bake**: Bake for 10-12 minutes until the crust is golden and the cheese is bubbly.
4. **Finish the pizza**: After baking, top with shredded lettuce and a drizzle of mayonnaise (optional).
5. **Serve**: Slice and enjoy!

Smoked Salmon Pizza

Ingredients:

- 1 pizza dough
- 1/2 cup crème fraîche or sour cream
- 1 1/2 cups shredded mozzarella cheese
- 1/2 lb smoked salmon, thinly sliced
- 1/4 cup red onion, thinly sliced
- Fresh dill for garnish
- 1 tbsp olive oil
- Lemon wedges for serving

Instructions:

1. **Preheat the oven**: Preheat to 475°F (245°C).
2. **Assemble the pizza**: Roll out the pizza dough and spread crème fraîche. Add mozzarella cheese, then top with smoked salmon and red onion slices.
3. **Bake**: Bake for 10-12 minutes until the crust is golden and cheese is melted.
4. **Finish the pizza**: Drizzle with olive oil and garnish with fresh dill.
5. **Serve**: Slice and serve with lemon wedges!

Taco Supreme Pizza

Ingredients:

- 1 pizza dough
- 1/2 cup salsa or taco sauce
- 1 1/2 cups shredded cheddar cheese
- 1/2 lb ground beef, cooked with taco seasoning
- 1/4 cup red onion, chopped
- 1/4 cup green bell pepper, chopped
- 1/2 cup black olives, sliced
- 1/4 cup sour cream (optional)
- Shredded lettuce for garnish

Instructions:

1. **Preheat the oven**: Preheat to 475°F (245°C).
2. **Assemble the pizza**: Roll out the pizza dough and spread salsa or taco sauce. Add cheddar cheese, cooked ground beef, red onion, bell pepper, and olives.
3. **Bake**: Bake for 10-12 minutes until the crust is golden and the cheese is melted.
4. **Finish the pizza**: After baking, top with sour cream and shredded lettuce.
5. **Serve**: Slice and enjoy!

Artichoke and Spinach Pizza

Ingredients:

- 1 pizza dough
- 1/2 cup Alfredo sauce or white pizza sauce
- 1 1/2 cups shredded mozzarella cheese
- 1/2 cup artichoke hearts, chopped
- 1/2 cup spinach, chopped
- 1/4 cup Parmesan cheese, grated
- 1 tbsp olive oil

Instructions:

1. **Preheat the oven**: Preheat to 475°F (245°C).
2. **Assemble the pizza**: Roll out the pizza dough and spread Alfredo sauce. Add mozzarella cheese, artichokes, and spinach.
3. **Bake**: Bake for 10-12 minutes until the crust is golden and the cheese is melted.
4. **Finish the pizza**: Sprinkle with Parmesan cheese and drizzle with olive oil.
5. **Serve**: Slice and enjoy!

Clam Pizza

Ingredients:

- 1 pizza dough
- 1/2 cup white pizza sauce (or olive oil and garlic)
- 1 1/2 cups shredded mozzarella cheese
- 1/2 lb canned or fresh clams, drained
- 2 cloves garlic, minced
- 1/4 cup Parmesan cheese, grated
- Fresh parsley for garnish

Instructions:

1. **Preheat the oven**: Preheat to 475°F (245°C).
2. **Assemble the pizza**: Roll out the pizza dough and spread white pizza sauce. Add mozzarella cheese, clams, and minced garlic.
3. **Bake**: Bake for 10-12 minutes until the crust is golden and the cheese is melted.
4. **Finish the pizza**: Sprinkle with Parmesan cheese and fresh parsley.
5. **Serve**: Slice and enjoy!

Focaccia-Style Pizza

Ingredients:

- 1 pizza dough
- 2 tbsp olive oil
- 1/2 cup rosemary, fresh and chopped
- 1/2 cup Parmesan cheese, grated
- 1/2 tsp coarse sea salt

Instructions:

1. **Preheat the oven**: Preheat to 475°F (245°C).
2. **Prepare the dough**: Roll out the pizza dough on a baking sheet. Drizzle with olive oil and press it gently with your fingers to create dimples in the dough.
3. **Assemble the pizza**: Sprinkle with rosemary, Parmesan cheese, and sea salt.
4. **Bake**: Bake for 10-12 minutes until golden and slightly crispy.
5. **Serve**: Slice and enjoy!

Mediterranean Veggie Pizza

Ingredients:

- 1 pizza dough
- 1/2 cup hummus or olive tapenade
- 1 1/2 cups shredded mozzarella cheese
- 1/2 cup Kalamata olives, pitted and sliced
- 1/2 cup cherry tomatoes, halved
- 1/2 red onion, thinly sliced
- 1/4 cup feta cheese, crumbled
- 1/4 cup fresh basil leaves
- 1 tbsp olive oil

Instructions:

1. **Preheat the oven**: Preheat to 475°F (245°C).
2. **Assemble the pizza**: Roll out the pizza dough and spread a layer of hummus or olive tapenade. Add mozzarella cheese, olives, tomatoes, red onion, and feta cheese.
3. **Bake**: Bake for 10-12 minutes until the crust is golden and the cheese is bubbly.
4. **Finish the pizza**: Drizzle with olive oil and top with fresh basil leaves.
5. **Serve**: Slice and enjoy!

Meatball Pizza

Ingredients:

- 1 pizza dough
- 1/2 cup marinara sauce
- 1 1/2 cups shredded mozzarella cheese
- 6-8 cooked meatballs, sliced
- 1/4 cup Parmesan cheese, grated
- 1/4 cup fresh basil, chopped

Instructions:

1. **Preheat the oven**: Preheat to 475°F (245°C).
2. **Assemble the pizza**: Roll out the pizza dough and spread marinara sauce. Add mozzarella cheese, sliced meatballs, and Parmesan cheese.
3. **Bake**: Bake for 10-12 minutes until the crust is golden and the cheese is melted.
4. **Finish the pizza**: Sprinkle with fresh basil.
5. **Serve**: Slice and enjoy!

Prosciutto and Arugula Pizza

Ingredients:

- 1 pizza dough
- 1/2 cup olive oil
- 1 1/2 cups shredded mozzarella cheese
- 6 slices prosciutto
- 1 cup fresh arugula
- 1 tbsp balsamic glaze

Instructions:

1. **Preheat the oven**: Preheat to 475°F (245°C).
2. **Assemble the pizza**: Roll out the pizza dough and drizzle with olive oil. Add mozzarella cheese.
3. **Bake**: Bake for 10-12 minutes until the crust is golden and the cheese is bubbly.
4. **Finish the pizza**: After baking, top with prosciutto, fresh arugula, and a drizzle of balsamic glaze.
5. **Serve**: Slice and enjoy!

Sweet and Spicy Pineapple Pizza

Ingredients:

- 1 pizza dough
- 1/2 cup pizza sauce or BBQ sauce
- 1 1/2 cups shredded mozzarella cheese
- 1/2 cup pineapple chunks
- 1/4 cup sliced red onion
- 1/4 cup jalapeño slices (optional for spice)
- 1 tbsp red pepper flakes (optional for extra heat)
- Fresh cilantro for garnish

Instructions:

1. **Preheat the oven**: Preheat to 475°F (245°C).
2. **Assemble the pizza**: Roll out the pizza dough and spread pizza sauce. Add mozzarella cheese, pineapple chunks, red onion, and jalapeños (if using).
3. **Bake**: Bake for 10-12 minutes until the crust is golden and the cheese is melted.
4. **Finish the pizza**: Sprinkle with red pepper flakes (optional) and fresh cilantro.
5. **Serve**: Slice and enjoy!

Zucchini and Feta Pizza

Ingredients:

- 1 pizza dough
- 1/2 cup olive oil
- 1 1/2 cups shredded mozzarella cheese
- 1/2 cup zucchini, thinly sliced
- 1/4 cup red onion, thinly sliced
- 1/4 cup crumbled feta cheese
- 1 tbsp fresh thyme leaves
- 1 tbsp lemon zest

Instructions:

1. **Preheat the oven**: Preheat to 475°F (245°C).
2. **Assemble the pizza**: Roll out the pizza dough and drizzle with olive oil. Add mozzarella cheese, zucchini, red onion, and feta cheese.
3. **Bake**: Bake for 10-12 minutes until the crust is golden and the cheese is melted.
4. **Finish the pizza**: Sprinkle with fresh thyme and lemon zest.
5. **Serve**: Slice and enjoy!

BBQ Bacon Cheeseburger Pizza

Ingredients:

- 1 pizza dough
- 1/2 cup BBQ sauce
- 1 1/2 cups shredded cheddar cheese
- 1/2 lb ground beef, cooked and seasoned
- 6 slices cooked bacon, crumbled
- 1/4 cup red onion, chopped
- 1/4 cup pickles, sliced
- 1 tbsp fresh cilantro

Instructions:

1. **Preheat the oven**: Preheat to 475°F (245°C).
2. **Assemble the pizza**: Roll out the pizza dough and spread BBQ sauce. Add cheddar cheese, cooked ground beef, crumbled bacon, and red onion.
3. **Bake**: Bake for 10-12 minutes until the crust is golden and the cheese is melted.
4. **Finish the pizza**: Top with pickles and fresh cilantro.
5. **Serve**: Slice and enjoy!

Roasted Veggie Pizza

Ingredients:

- 1 pizza dough
- 1/2 cup pizza sauce
- 1 1/2 cups shredded mozzarella cheese
- 1/2 cup roasted bell peppers, sliced
- 1/2 cup roasted mushrooms, sliced
- 1/4 cup roasted zucchini, sliced
- 1/4 cup Parmesan cheese, grated
- Fresh basil for garnish

Instructions:

1. **Preheat the oven**: Preheat to 475°F (245°C).
2. **Assemble the pizza**: Roll out the pizza dough and spread pizza sauce. Add mozzarella cheese, roasted bell peppers, mushrooms, and zucchini.
3. **Bake**: Bake for 10-12 minutes until the crust is golden and the cheese is melted.
4. **Finish the pizza**: Sprinkle with Parmesan cheese and garnish with fresh basil.
5. **Serve**: Slice and enjoy!

Steak and Gorgonzola Pizza

Ingredients:

- 1 pizza dough
- 1/2 cup olive oil
- 1 1/2 cups shredded mozzarella cheese
- 1/2 lb cooked steak, thinly sliced
- 1/4 cup Gorgonzola cheese, crumbled
- 1/4 cup red onion, thinly sliced
- Fresh arugula for garnish

Instructions:

1. **Preheat the oven**: Preheat to 475°F (245°C).
2. **Assemble the pizza**: Roll out the pizza dough and drizzle with olive oil. Add mozzarella cheese, steak slices, Gorgonzola cheese, and red onion.
3. **Bake**: Bake for 10-12 minutes until the crust is golden and the cheese is melted.
4. **Finish the pizza**: Garnish with fresh arugula.
5. **Serve**: Slice and enjoy!

Eggplant Parmesan Pizza

Ingredients:

- 1 pizza dough
- 1/2 cup marinara sauce
- 1 1/2 cups shredded mozzarella cheese
- 1/2 cup Parmesan cheese, grated
- 1 small eggplant, thinly sliced
- 1/4 cup fresh basil leaves

Instructions:

1. **Preheat the oven**: Preheat to 475°F (245°C).
2. **Prepare the eggplant**: Slice eggplant and roast or grill until tender.
3. **Assemble the pizza**: Roll out the pizza dough and spread marinara sauce. Add mozzarella cheese, roasted eggplant slices, and Parmesan cheese.
4. **Bake**: Bake for 10-12 minutes until the crust is golden and the cheese is bubbly.
5. **Finish the pizza**: Top with fresh basil.
6. **Serve**: Slice and enjoy!

Ricotta and Sausage Pizza

Ingredients:

- 1 pizza dough
- 1/2 cup marinara sauce
- 1 1/2 cups shredded mozzarella cheese
- 1/2 cup ricotta cheese
- 1/2 lb Italian sausage, cooked and crumbled
- 1/4 cup Parmesan cheese, grated
- Fresh basil for garnish

Instructions:

1. **Preheat the oven**: Preheat to 475°F (245°C).
2. **Assemble the pizza**: Roll out the pizza dough and spread marinara sauce. Add mozzarella cheese, ricotta cheese, cooked sausage, and Parmesan cheese.
3. **Bake**: Bake for 10-12 minutes until the crust is golden and the cheese is melted.
4. **Finish the pizza**: Garnish with fresh basil.
5. **Serve**: Slice and enjoy!

Gorgonzola, Pear, and Walnut Pizza

Ingredients:

- 1 pizza dough
- 1/2 cup olive oil
- 1 1/2 cups shredded mozzarella cheese
- 1/2 cup Gorgonzola cheese, crumbled
- 1 pear, thinly sliced
- 1/4 cup walnuts, chopped
- 1 tbsp honey
- Fresh arugula for garnish

Instructions:

1. **Preheat the oven**: Preheat to 475°F (245°C).
2. **Assemble the pizza**: Roll out the pizza dough and drizzle with olive oil. Add mozzarella cheese, Gorgonzola cheese, pear slices, and walnuts.
3. **Bake**: Bake for 10-12 minutes until the crust is golden and the cheese is bubbly.
4. **Finish the pizza**: Drizzle with honey and garnish with fresh arugula.
5. **Serve**: Slice and enjoy!

Balsamic Glazed Onion Pizza

Ingredients:

- 1 pizza dough
- 1/2 cup pizza sauce
- 1 1/2 cups shredded mozzarella cheese
- 1 onion, thinly sliced
- 1 tbsp olive oil
- 1 tbsp balsamic vinegar
- Fresh thyme for garnish

Instructions:

1. **Preheat the oven**: Preheat to 475°F (245°C).
2. **Caramelize the onions**: In a skillet, heat olive oil over medium heat and cook the onions until soft and caramelized (about 10 minutes). Add balsamic vinegar and cook for an additional 2 minutes.
3. **Assemble the pizza**: Roll out the pizza dough and spread pizza sauce. Add mozzarella cheese and top with caramelized onions.
4. **Bake**: Bake for 10-12 minutes until the crust is golden and the cheese is melted.
5. **Finish the pizza**: Garnish with fresh thyme.
6. **Serve**: Slice and enjoy!

Fig and Prosciutto Pizza

Ingredients:

- 1 pizza dough
- 1/2 cup pizza sauce or olive oil
- 1 1/2 cups shredded mozzarella cheese
- 1/2 cup fresh figs, sliced
- 6 slices prosciutto
- 1 tbsp honey
- Fresh arugula for garnish

Instructions:

1. **Preheat the oven**: Preheat to 475°F (245°C).
2. **Assemble the pizza**: Roll out the pizza dough and spread pizza sauce or olive oil. Add mozzarella cheese and arrange sliced figs on top.
3. **Bake**: Bake for 10-12 minutes until the crust is golden and the cheese is bubbly.
4. **Finish the pizza**: Top with prosciutto, drizzle with honey, and garnish with fresh arugula.
5. **Serve**: Slice and enjoy!

Goat Cheese and Caramelized Onion Pizza

Ingredients:

- 1 pizza dough
- 1/2 cup olive oil
- 1 1/2 cups shredded mozzarella cheese
- 1/2 cup goat cheese, crumbled
- 1 onion, thinly sliced
- 1 tbsp honey
- Fresh rosemary for garnish

Instructions:

1. **Preheat the oven**: Preheat to 475°F (245°C).
2. **Caramelize the onions**: In a skillet, heat olive oil over medium heat and cook the onions until soft and caramelized (about 10 minutes). Add honey and cook for another 2 minutes.
3. **Assemble the pizza**: Roll out the pizza dough and drizzle with olive oil. Add mozzarella cheese, goat cheese, and caramelized onions.
4. **Bake**: Bake for 10-12 minutes until the crust is golden and the cheese is melted.
5. **Finish the pizza**: Garnish with fresh rosemary.
6. **Serve**: Slice and enjoy!

Roasted Garlic and Herb Pizza

Ingredients:

- 1 pizza dough
- 1/2 cup olive oil
- 1 1/2 cups shredded mozzarella cheese
- 1/4 cup roasted garlic cloves, mashed
- 1 tbsp fresh rosemary, chopped
- 1 tbsp fresh thyme, chopped
- Parmesan cheese for garnish

Instructions:

1. **Preheat the oven**: Preheat to 475°F (245°C).
2. **Roast the garlic**: Roast the garlic by wrapping it in foil and baking at 400°F (200°C) for 20 minutes, until soft. Mash the cloves.
3. **Assemble the pizza**: Roll out the pizza dough and drizzle with olive oil. Spread mashed roasted garlic and add mozzarella cheese. Sprinkle with rosemary and thyme.
4. **Bake**: Bake for 10-12 minutes until the crust is golden and the cheese is melted.
5. **Finish the pizza**: Garnish with Parmesan cheese.
6. **Serve**: Slice and enjoy!

Pesto Chicken and Sun-Dried Tomato Pizza

Ingredients:

- 1 pizza dough
- 1/2 cup pesto sauce
- 1 1/2 cups shredded mozzarella cheese
- 1/2 cup cooked chicken, shredded
- 1/4 cup sun-dried tomatoes, chopped
- Fresh basil for garnish

Instructions:

1. **Preheat the oven**: Preheat to 475°F (245°C).
2. **Assemble the pizza**: Roll out the pizza dough and spread pesto sauce. Add mozzarella cheese, shredded chicken, and sun-dried tomatoes.
3. **Bake**: Bake for 10-12 minutes until the crust is golden and the cheese is bubbly.
4. **Finish the pizza**: Garnish with fresh basil.
5. **Serve**: Slice and enjoy!

Roasted Beetroot and Goat Cheese Pizza

Ingredients:

- 1 pizza dough
- 1/2 cup olive oil
- 1 1/2 cups shredded mozzarella cheese
- 1/2 cup roasted beetroot, sliced
- 1/4 cup goat cheese, crumbled
- 1 tbsp balsamic vinegar
- Fresh arugula for garnish

Instructions:

1. **Preheat the oven**: Preheat to 475°F (245°C).
2. **Assemble the pizza**: Roll out the pizza dough and drizzle with olive oil. Add mozzarella cheese, roasted beetroot, and goat cheese.
3. **Bake**: Bake for 10-12 minutes until the crust is golden and the cheese is melted.
4. **Finish the pizza**: Drizzle with balsamic vinegar and garnish with fresh arugula.
5. **Serve**: Slice and enjoy!

Truffle Mushroom Pizza

Ingredients:

- 1 pizza dough
- 1/2 cup olive oil
- 1 1/2 cups shredded mozzarella cheese
- 1/2 lb mixed mushrooms, thinly sliced
- 1 tbsp truffle oil
- Fresh thyme for garnish

Instructions:

1. **Preheat the oven**: Preheat to 475°F (245°C).
2. **Sauté the mushrooms**: In a skillet, heat olive oil over medium heat and sauté the mushrooms until soft (about 5 minutes).
3. **Assemble the pizza**: Roll out the pizza dough and drizzle with olive oil. Add mozzarella cheese and sautéed mushrooms.
4. **Bake**: Bake for 10-12 minutes until the crust is golden and the cheese is melted.
5. **Finish the pizza**: Drizzle with truffle oil and garnish with fresh thyme.
6. **Serve**: Slice and enjoy!

www.ingramcontent.com/pod-product-compliance
Lightning Source LLC
LaVergne TN
LVHW061955070526
838199LV00060B/4127

9798330571789